# Teacher's Gui
# Children

**Janet Kay**

## continuum
LONDON • NEW YORK

**Continuum**
The Tower Building
11 York Road
London SE1 7NX
*www.continuumbooks.com*

15 East 26th Street
New York
NY 10010

*British Library Cataloguing-in-Publication Data*
A catalogue record for this book is available from the British Library.

ISBN 08264 6637 0

Typeset by Originator Publishing Services
Printed in Great Britain by Biddles Ltd, Guildford and King's Lynn

# Contents

# Contents

# Series Introduction

*Dear Teacher*

Classmates is an exciting and innovative new series developed by Continuum, and is designed to help you improve your teaching, and your career.

With your huge workload, both inside and outside of school, we understand that you have less time to read around your profession. These short, pithy guides have been designed with an accessible layout so that you do not have to wade through lots of dull, heavy text to find the information you need.

All of our authors have first-hand teaching experience and have written this essential series with busy teachers in mind. Our subjects range from taking school trips (*Tips for Trips*) and dealing with parents (*Involving Parents*) to coping with the large amounts of stress in your life (*Stress Busting*) and creating more personal time for yourself (*Every Minute Counts*).

If you have practical advice that you would like to share with your fellow teachers and think that you could write a book for this series, then we would be delighted to hear from you.

We do hope that you enjoy reading our *Classmates*. With very best wishes

*Continuum's Education Team*

P.S. Watch out for our second batch of ten *Classmates*, to be launched in March 2004.

**1**

# Protecting children: the role of teachers

## Introduction

Teachers and other school staff have more contact with a wider range of children than other professionals and, as such, are ideally placed to recognize and respond to cases of child abuse when they arise. Yet current research indicates that many teachers feel that they simply do not have the skills and knowledge to respond effectively to incidents of possible abuse. Despite the raised profile of education services in the child protection process, many teachers have received only the minimum of training, or no training at all, and very few have opportunity to access joint training with other child protection professionals.

Teachers often report confusion and anxiety over what is expected of them within the legal and procedural framework supporting the child protection process. Some research shows that teachers lack confidence in recognizing possible indicators of abuse, and that relationships with other child protection professionals can sometimes be characterized by mutual lack of understanding and even lack of professional respect.

# Teacher's Guide to Protecting Children

New guidelines and procedures in child protection can be seen as an additional burden to teaching staff already overwhelmed with continuing developments in education. Yet in recent years there has been a sustained drive to widen the responsibility for protecting children to include non-social services agencies, particularly health and education, and to deliver child protection services through a multi-agency approach. This drive continues with the *Victoria Climbie Inquiry Report* (January 2003), which makes a number of recommendations that will 'alter how schools and education authorities help to protect children'. For example:

> *The Teacher Training Agency should ensure teachers are trained to work effectively and share information with police, social workers and other public services staff.*
>
> (Shaw, 31/1/03)

There has probably never been a more crucial time for teachers to raise their awareness of, and confidence in, dealing with child abuse and the child protection process. However, despite the increased emphasis on the role of schools in child protection, the *Climbie Inquiry Report* has been criticized for not recognizing that schools can play a much more central role in promoting inter-agency co-operation than has previously been achieved (Revell, 7/2/03). For example, the recent development of 'full-service' schools in Norfolk, providing family-centred support services delivered by health, education and social services, attempts to eradicate some of the existing and pernicious barriers to genuine 'working together' (www.infed.org/schooling/f-se4v.htm).

It is clear that schools have a significant and developing role in the protection of children, not always supported by the level of training and expertise that teachers have in this area. This short book is intended to offer teaching staff an accessible and easy-to-read guide to their role in the child protection process, which can be used for reference as child protection issues arise as well as being read as a whole. It is intended for heads and teachers, teaching assistants and other school staff with direct responsibility for children, Child Protection Liaison teachers, and staff and students on initial teacher training courses. The book is divided into sub-sections addressing key areas of knowledge and skills in the child protection process and outlining the roles and responsibilities of teaching staff within these.

To avoid using he/she or other such combinations, 'he' and 'she' are used randomly throughout. The term 'parent' is used to describe anyone with parental responsibility for a child. The term 'teachers' is used to describe teachers, teaching assistants, student teachers and anyone else with direct responsibility for children within schools.

References and a further reading list, including key child protection documents, can be found at the end of the book.

## Recognizing child abuse

One of the key roles of teaching staff in child protection is to recognize and respond to evidence that a child in their care may be being abused. Yet for many teachers, this raises the question: 'How do I know if abuse has really taken place?' Recognition involves developing the skills and knowledge needed to identify the indicators of possible abuse in individual children. Responses to possible abuse situations are discussed in the next section.

There are many documented cases of child abuse which cite the failure of professionals to recognize the indicators of abuse as a key factor in the child's death. The *Victoria Climbie Inquiry Report* (January 2003) concluded that Victoria's death was partly a result of the failure of professionals from a number of agencies involved in child protection to recognize that her many injuries were the result of abuse. The report cites 12 key opportunities when various professionals could have recognized that abuse was taking place and saved Victoria's life. The ability to recognize and respond to possible abuse is a key skill in child protection work and the main child protection responsibility of professionals working directly with children in schools.

Teachers take a central role with children aged three and above, having more opportunity to monitor their behaviour and condition than any other professionals working with this age group. And yet research shows that many teachers lack confidence in their own ability to recognize the indicators of abuse reliably, and that a lack of training and staff development in this area means that many teachers do not have a clear understanding of what child abuse is, or how it can be identified. Baginsky (2000: 3) found, in a survey of schools, that 88 per cent of respondents did not feel confident that all teachers would be able to recognize and respond to the signs of abuse. Despite this, more child abuse referrals come from schools than from any other agency working with children. Dealing with the responsibility of this key role can feel very stressful for individual teaching staff and this may lead to anxiety about how to respond to suspected abuse. This section focuses on the key factors that would lead you to believe that abuse may have taken place.

## Definitions and indicators of child abuse

There are many and varied definitions of child abuse, which have changed over time as our understanding of what is abusive to children has developed and become more complex. The definitions currently used are those set out within the *Working Together to Safeguard Children* (DoH, 1999) guidelines. This key government document includes procedural guidelines for all professionals in identifying and responding to child abuse, including staff in all educational settings. You can find it on the Department of Health website at www.doh. gov.uk

Definitions of abuse can be useful because they give us a starting point for recognizing behaviours towards children that are deemed unacceptable within our society at a certain point in time. Definitions of abuse can change because they are defined by cultural norms within particular societies. As such, definitions are dynamic and will alter over time. Types of punishments and behaviours towards children that were commonplace 20, 30 or 50 years ago may well be looked upon as wholly unacceptable in the 21st century. For example, the use of smacking as a punishment has receded within institutional settings over the last 30 years, and recent bids to legislate against smacking within the family have signalled ongoing change in this area.

Child abuse is currently defined within four categories: physical, sexual, emotional and neglectful. These categories are useful for analysis, but quite clearly overlap, with many common indicators. Many children suffer from more than one type of abuse. For example, children suffering physical or sexual abuse may well also experience emotional harm through the low value that they perceive is placed on them by their abusers.

Department of Health statistics show the patterns of change in the numbers and proportions of children registered in each category. These figures relate to children who have had their names placed on the Child Protection Register after a child protection case conference. It is important to remember that the figures reflect only known and investigated cases of abuse, rather than the 'real' picture, which may include many more abused children who have gone unnoticed.

At the end of March, 2001 in England:

> *there were 26,800 children's names on child protection registers; 70 per cent of registered children were under 10; 46 per cent of children were registered in the category for neglect; 30 per cent for physical injury; 16 percent for sexual abuse; 17 per cent for emotional abuse; and 52 per cent of registered children were boys and 48 per cent were girls.* (DoH, March 2001)

The figures highlight the role of primary schools in particular in identifying and responding to abuse affecting young children aged three to 10.

## *Physical abuse*

The physical abuse of children is perhaps the most commonly understood type of abuse. Although the abuse of children has been documented from almost the beginning of history, our recent awareness of the nature and extent of physical abuse of children within the family stems from the work of Henry Kempe and his colleagues in the 1960s. Through their recognition of what they initially called 'the battered baby' syndrome, Kempe and his colleagues publicized the widespread nature of child abuse and considerably raised public awareness of the issues.

The current government definition of physical abuse is:

> *Physical abuse may involve hitting, shaking, throwing, poisoning, burning or scalding, drowning, suffocating, or otherwise causing physical harm to a child. Physical harm may also be caused when a parent or carer feigns the symptoms of, or deliberately causes, ill health to a child whom they are looking after. This situation is commonly described using terms such as factitious illness by proxy or Munchausen syndrome by proxy.*  (DoH, 1999: 2.4)

Recognizing physical abuse usually involves becoming aware of a pattern of injuries affecting the child, although single serious injuries should alert you to possible abuse. The injuries may seem unlikely to have been caused accidentally: for example, if they include bruises that show the shape of implements, knuckles or fingertips. They may include injuries to the face such as bruised eyes and cheeks, and injuries to soft tissues such as buttocks and thighs. The key indicator may be the discrepancy between the injury and the explanation for the injury, or multiple conflicting explanations from the parent and child. The scale and severity of injuries may escalate over time. The child may try to conceal the injury or avoid being questioned about it. The parent may not take the child for medical treatment when this is clearly indicated. There may also be a pattern of unexplained absences from school.

For example, a girl of seven appeared in school with bruises to her face on several occasions. The teacher became concerned when the child told conflicting stories about how these were caused. When the teacher raised concerns with the parent, the child stopped coming to school for a week. Checking the register, it became apparent the child had not attended school on PE days for a long time, and later it became apparent that this was to conceal bruises and cigarette burns which were found on her body and legs.

Recent cases such as Victoria Climbie and Lauren Wright have highlighted the plausibility of some physically abusive parents. In both cases, injuries were not identified as abuse because the parent asserted that they had been caused accidentally and this was believed. It is important to be aware that abuse does take place in all types of families and not to dismiss this as a possible explanation for any injury to any child.

Indicators of physical abuse may include:

♦ unexplained injuries or injuries where there are conflicting explanations

♦ a repeated pattern of injuries which seem unlikely to

have been caused accidentally, e.g. bruises at different stages of healing

♦ scalds and burns with clear outlines

♦ bite marks

♦ bruising to the face, black eyes; bruising to the buttocks and torso

♦ fingertip bruising, hand marks, grasp marks and marks of implements

♦ untreated internal injuries or broken bones

♦ child conceals or is reluctant to discuss injuries

♦ withdrawn or aggressive behaviour, loss of confidence, social problems or lack of achievement in school.

## *Emotional abuse*

Emotional neglect involves the failure of parents to meet the child's need for love, security, positive regard, warmth, praise and a sense of 'belongingness' in their family and the wider world. Emotional neglect may be associated with a failure to respond to the child's basic needs or with a parent who is 'psychologically unavailable' to the child – in other words, a parent who is unresponsive to the child's needs because he/she does not recognize them. An emotionally neglected child may have insecure attachments within the family and as a result may suffer from poor self-esteem, delays in development and difficulties in social relationships. Emotional neglect may be accompanied by other sorts of neglect, such as failure to meet the child's basic physical needs on a consistent basis, and failure to ensure the child is safe and secure through proper supervision.

Emotional abuse is a more active assault on the child's emotional and psychological well-being. It may involve selecting the child for ridicule and verbal abuse, shaming the child, treating the child as unwanted and unloved, forcing the child to perform tasks for food and comfort, or locking the child in a room alone. For example, in one case, a five-year-old boy was forced to sleep on the floor, told every day that he wasn't wanted or loved, refused food if he misbehaved, and never touched or picked up by his mother. His two sisters were treated as loved and cherished children. The boy became very distressed, wetting and soiling at school, and ripping wallpaper and setting it on fire at home.

*Working Together to Safeguard Children* (DoH, 1999: 2.5) gives a definition of emotional abuse as follows:

> *Emotional abuse is the persistent emotional ill treatment of a child such as to cause severe and persistent adverse effects on the child's emotional development. It may involve conveying to children that they are worthless or unloved, inadequate, or valued only insofar as they meet the needs of another person. It may feature age or developmentally inappropriate expectations being imposed on children. It may involve causing children frequently to feel frightened or in danger, or the exploitation or corruption of children. Some level of emotional*

*abuse is involved in all types of ill-treatment of a child, though it may occur alone.*

Recognizing emotional abuse and neglect involves observing and monitoring the child's behaviour. Emotionally neglected and abused children usually have very low self-esteem. They may lack confidence to tackle their tasks in school and may respond emotionally under pressure. They may seek inappropriately close relationships with staff, or draw attention to themselves through unwanted behaviour. Alternatively, the child may be withdrawn and sad, unable to join in and socially isolated. Emotionally abused children may demonstrate neurotic behaviour at times, such as pulling out their own hair or self-harming. They may have bursts of anger or distress, or complete withdrawal. On the other hand, the child may by over-compliant and trying too hard to please. Emotional abuse and neglect may occur alone or as part of a more complex abusive situation. For example, the relationship between sexual and emotional abuse is well documented.

Indicators of emotional abuse and neglect may include:

*[handwritten: Indicatos of emotional abuse]*

♦ Chronic lack of self-esteem and low self-confidence

♦ Immature emotional responses, regression and neurotic behaviour

♦ Demanding behaviour, attention-seeking, inappropriate behaviour towards non-parental adults

- ◆ Withdrawn behaviour, failure to make friends or sustain friendships

- ◆ Fear of new tasks, not wanting to experiment or join in

- ◆ Developmental and learning delays

- ◆ Outbursts of anger or distress

- ◆ Indifferent or negative relationship with parents

- ◆ Over-compliant behaviour, excessive desire to please.

## *Sexual abuse*

The extent and nature of the sexual abuse of children was little understood before the 1980s, when it became apparent through the work of a range of professionals in the field that sexual abuse of children was much more common and widespread than previously believed. The secret and taboo nature of child sexual abuse within the family meant that many cases never came to light prior to this, and, worse still, many others were dismissed or not responded to by the professionals involved. Many sexually abused children never received the support and help they needed to help them with the trauma they suffered, and grew to adulthood without sharing their secret.

Now it is widely recognized that sexual abuse within the family is common compared to stranger abuse, with the majority of children, both boys and girls, abused by close male relatives. The debate about child sexual abuse over the last two decades has erased some of the taboos surrounding this type of abuse and raised awareness among professionals and the public alike. However, child sexual abuse remains a secret act, often only known to the child and the abuser. Successful prosecutions of perpetrators continue at a low rate, and many cases are suspected but not proven. A number of widely reported cases in the 1990s highlighted the dangers of child sexual abuse within institutional settings, particularly those which were meant to provide a safe and secure environment for children already suffering from abuse.

Sexual abuse of children can take many forms including using pornography to stimulate children sexually, child prostitution, abuse by groups of adults and making pornographic material for distribution to others. Sexual abuse can involve coercion, violent attack, threats and intimidation. It can also occur within an apparently loving relationship where the child is gradually introduced to sexual activity through a series of small steps, progressing towards penetrative sex. This is sometimes described as 'grooming'.

Recent developments include an increased recognition of the role of children in abusing other children, particularly within the family. The NSPCC survey *Child Maltreatment in the United Kingdom* (NSPCC, November 2000) found a much greater prevalence of sibling abuse than had been previously recognized. The child abused was usually a sister or step-sister, the abuser usually a brother or step-brother. Brothers were found to be responsible for more than one-third of sexual abuse committed by relatives (*Independent on Sunday*, 19/11/2000). The NSPCC survey also found that children under 10 who abuse have usually been sexually abused themselves. However, boys who have reached puberty and who sexually abuse have often been physically abused themselves. For example, in one case, a 13-year-old boy, who had been physically and sexually abused by his uncle from the age of five, became involved in abusing his younger siblings and later sexually assaulted other children within a residential unit. *Working Together to Safeguard Children* (DoH, 1999: 2.6), defines child sexual abuse of children as follows:

> *Sexual abuse involves forcing or enticing a child or young person to take part in sexual activities, whether or not the child is aware of what is happening. The activities may involve physical contact, including penetrative (e.g. rape or buggery) or non-penetrative acts. They may include non-contact activities, such as involving children in looking at, or in the production of, pornographic material or watching sexual activities, or encouraging children to behave in sexually inappropriate ways.*

Recognizing child sexual abuse can be difficult unless the child 'discloses' the abuse by telling an adult about it. Although this can and does happen, the child may find it difficult to talk to others about the sexual abuse if it has been accompanied by threats of violence or separation from non-abusing family members.

Many children who are sexually abused will show signs of emotional abuse as described above. The child may perceive herself as worthless and unlovable, valuable only in terms of the extent to which she can satisfy adult sexual needs. The impact of the emotionally abusive aspects of the sexual abuse may last longer and have more negative implications for the child than any physical consequences. Depending on the type and severity of the sexual abuse, not all children will show physical symptoms. However, for some children the physical consequence can be very severe in terms of diseases such as hepatitis, HIV, gonorrhoea and syphilis, physical damage to the reproductive organs or pregnancy.

One of the common indicators of child sexual abuse is inappropriate sexual knowledge and behaviour in the child. This goes far beyond the normal curiosity and experimentation that every child involves himself in during different stages of sexual development. It may involve persistently introducing sexual themes into conversation, play and art work, sexual attacks or sexually coercive play with other children, and sexualized behaviour with adults. For example, one school reported that there seemed to have been an outbreak of sexual abuse involving many children. However, on investigation it became clear that only two children within one family had been sexually abused. They had introduced the other children to some highly sexualized play themes and conversations, and this is what staff had observed in school.

Indicators of child sexual abuse may include:

♦ Bruising and/or bite marks around the genital area, bottom or thighs

♦ Unusual bleeding or discharge from the genitals

♦ Inappropriate sexual behaviour towards adults and/or other children

- Sexual knowledge inappropriate for the child's age
- Self-harming
- Eating and sleeping disturbances
- Depression, low self-esteem, suicidal behaviour
- Poor achievements in school.

## *Neglect*

Identifying a child who is neglected can seem particularly difficult. How can we tell the difference between wilful neglect and the consequences of poverty within the family? It is important to recognize that neglect is only partially about the level of financial resources within the family. More significantly, it is about the proportion of resources that are channelled towards meeting the child's needs. Resources can include, money, goods, time, energy and space. The child's needs are physical, emotional, social and developmental. Neglect occurs where the child's needs have low priority within the family and therefore there is little or no attempt to meet them to any acceptable extent. The child may be neglected through lack of appropriate nutrition; poor levels of developmental activities such as play, adult time and attention, stimulation and conversation; lack of responsiveness and warmth from the parent; and failure to ensure the child's safety through good levels of hygiene, supervision and medical attention. This does not mean that every parent who forgets a dental appointment or watches the football instead of reading with their child is neglectful! Neglect is persistent and ongoing, and ultimately measured by the extent to which it has a negative impact on the child's health and development.

*Working Together to Safeguard Children* (DoH, 1999: 2.7) defines neglect thus:

> *Neglect is the persistent failure to meet a child's basic physical and/or psychological needs, likely to result in the serious impairment of the child's health or development. It may involve a parent or carer failing to provide adequate food, shelter and clothing, failing to protect a child from physical harm or danger, or the failure to ensure access to appropriate medical care or treatment. It may also include neglect of, or unresponsiveness to, a child's basic emotional needs.*

This definition includes emotional neglect as discussed earlier in this section.

Identifying neglect is likely to be an ongoing process over a period of time. Evidence of neglect may come from the child's appearance and behaviour, the parent's behaviour and attitude towards the child, and assessment of the child's developmental and educational progress. A neglected child may show failure to thrive, which adversely affects the child's growth and weight. This can be demonstrated through health assessments that exclude other organic causes of failure to thrive, as not all failure to thrive is caused by neglect. However, a child who is failing to thrive where no health assessment has taken place should be a cause for concern.

Neglected children may appear thin and pale, have poor hygiene, and be hungry and tired. They may be late to school or have frequent unexplained absences. Their clothing may be inadequate for the weather conditions, and often dirty and smelly. The child may not be achieving in school, may have learning delays and lack motivation to take part in tasks. Social relationships may be poor, and the child may be socially rejected. There may be a lack of appropriate social knowledge and lack of self-control or disturbances in the child's behaviour. Neglected children often have untreated medical conditions, and may be more prone to accidents due to lack of adequate supervision. For example, in one case the child suffered repeated middle ear infections, which, having been left untreated despite the efforts of the health professionals involved, resulted in permanent hearing loss.

The parents may show indifference or lack of response to the child and the child's needs. They may avoid contact with school, or react negatively to attempts to discuss the child's progress. The child may be collected and delivered to school by an ever-changing range of different adults.

Indicators of neglect may include:

♦ poor growth and development, failure to thrive without an organic cause

♦ failing to achieve in school, learning delays

♦ poor hygiene, inadequate clothing

♦ untreated medical conditions

♦ poor self-esteem

♦ chronic tiredness and hunger, falling asleep in class, voracious eating

- mottled purplish skin, sores, poor hair condition
- lateness to school, frequent non-attendance
- poor social relationships, indiscriminate attention-seeking with adults
- high level of accidents.

# Disclosure

Child abuse may not always come to light because indicators have been identified. Sometimes children disclose abuse to adults they trust within the school or other 'safe' environments. The child may simply tell you that he is being abused, or may hint at this during activities or play. The two issues to consider in preparation for disclosure are how to respond to the child and how to manage the situation within a school setting.

Responding to the child requires patience and sensitivity. It is important to recognize that the child has chosen you because she trusts you and feels that you have the ability to help her. The way in which disclosure is responded to may have a significant impact on how the child copes with the subsequent investigation and procedural and legal responses. If a child discloses abuse to you, you should: seek a private place where interruptions can be minimized; listen carefully, without interrupting or asking questions; reassure the child and be comforting; avoid promising not to tell others; and record the conversations as soon as possible.

But what if the child starts to disclose in front of a whole class? It may be very difficult to seek a private place if you have 33 other children for whom you are responsible. This can only be resolved at school level and it is important that you are aware of how disclosure is managed on a school-wide basis. One primary school manages disclosure through a card system. Every teacher has a red card in his desk which can be sent with another child or adult to the school office, thereby summoning another adult to come to the class and take over while the teacher continues with the disclosure in private.

# Issues and problems in identifying child abuse

## Other explanations for possible indicators of abuse

The ability to identify child abuse goes far beyond comparing the child's behaviour and appearance with a checklist of indicators. Many of the behavioural indicators could have other, non-abusive causes. Some of these could include: divorce or separation of parents; domestic abuse within the household; bereavement; birth of a sibling; becoming part of a step-family or gaining a new step-parent; moving house, changing neighbourhood; and long-term or acute physical or mental illness of a sibling or parent.

It is important to be aware of other factors influencing a child's behaviour before concluding that abuse is the only possible explanation. However, changes occurring in a child's family situation could indicate

20

that the child may be becoming more vulnerable to abuse. For example, it used to be believed that children in households where domestic abuse was a regular event were not necessarily abused. However, we now know much more about the emotional damage that children who grow up in violent households suffer from and the disruptions they may experience in their lives.

## Identifying causes for concern

Identifying abuse involves recognizing patterns of events taking place in connection with the child, and recognizing a range of relevant indicators, often over a period of time. Single indicators are usually unlikely to be adequate in confirming suspicions of abuse, but in a small number of cases single injuries or indicators of sexual assault may be significant. Changes in the appearance and behaviour of the child are often significant, especially if linked with changes in family structure or situation.

Important issues include:

♦ keeping records of events or concerns about the child over time

♦ discussing concerns with parents and monitoring their reaction

♦ monitoring the child's appearance and behaviour

♦ recognizing the need to exclude other explanations for possible indicators of abuse (see above)

- ♦ identifying a range of physical and behavioural indicators, possibly over time

- ♦ checking colleagues' perceptions and concerns in confidence

- ♦ seeking advice and support from more experienced colleagues in confidence

- ♦ recognizing that all children from all types of families can be abused

- ♦ acknowledging that some abusers can be socially adept, plausible and skilful liars

- ♦ taking into account that each child is an individual in a unique situation.

## *Factors affecting the recognition of child abuse*

The main factors that influence your ability to recognize and respond to child abuse lie in your knowledge and understanding of the children in your care and your ability to observe and interpret their appearance and behaviour effectively. However, there are a number of factors which can make it difficult to develop and exercise skills in observation and identification of problems with the children in your care:

- ♦ lack of time with individual children in large classes

- ♦ focus on covering curriculum subjects during teaching time

- ♦ paperwork absorbing non-teaching time in schools

♦ lack of training for all staff in child protection issues

♦ fear of allegations against yourself

♦ the belief that child protection is someone else's remit

♦ fear of getting involved, getting it wrong, making the situation worse

♦ fear of retribution from aggrieved parents.

It is important to acknowledge that these factors can be very real deterrents to effective child protection and can create a situation where indicators of abuse are ignored or not recognized. However, the Children Act 1989 placed a responsibility on all professionals working with children to ensure their protection from abuse and teachers have a remit to ensure that they understand what is required from them and their school in this area.

## *Recognizing abuse of individual children*

We all may have an image of the 'abused child', possible a thin, forlorn and waiflike figure. But in reality, the abused child may be the aggressive class bully or the quiet child who never causes a stir in the classroom. There are no boundaries to the types of children who may be being abused. Similarly, parents who abuse are not all obvious to those around them.

Recognizing abuse must be based on observation and reflection about a child's condition and behaviour rather than perceptions or assumptions about different children's family lives. Some, but not all, children may be more vulnerable to abuse because of: disability or learning difficulties; communication or language delays; alcohol or drug abuse within the family; domestic violence within the family; mental illness of a parent; and social isolation of the family.

However, it would be a dangerous assumption to believe that all children in these categories are potentially abused or that children outside these categories will not be abused.

# Checklist for action

1. Check the availability within your school of the school child protection procedures, the LEA Child Protection Procedures and the Area Child Protection Committee Child Protection Procedures and familiarize yourself with their description of your role in child protection.

2. Make sure you know who the Child Protection Liaison teacher is within your school.

3. Ask about training in child protection within the LEA or for staff within the school, including joint training events with other professionals.

4. Check school procedures to be followed if a child begins to disclose abuse in class.

**2**

# Responding to suspected child abuse

## Introduction

Once you believe that there is a possibility that a child of whom you have knowledge may be being abused, it is important to be clear about the procedures that must then be followed. Child protection procedures provide a common framework to guide the responses of all professionals involved in any such enquiry, and to ensure that the child and family are dealt with appropriately. In each local authority, the Area Child Protection Committee (ACPC) has the responsibility for producing child protection procedures, based on the *Working Together to Safeguard Children* (DoH, 1999) guidelines. These procedures describe the roles of all professionals involved with children and incorporate the principles of the Children Act 1989, as described in the section on 'Legal and Procedural Issues'. Your school should also have its own child protection procedures.

Following procedure at this stage is crucial in ensuring that an enquiry, including any legal action, is successful in supporting the child and family and ensuring the child's future safety. Professionals involved with children are encouraged to recognize that their role in child protection is not voluntary, but part of their more general professional roles and responsibilities. In other words, you do not have a choice as to whether to act or not in this situation. If there is evidence that could lead to a conclusion of child abuse, you must take steps to instigate an enquiry.

# Referring suspected abuse

Despite the guidelines and policies available on child protection procedures, Baginsky (2000: 3) found that two-thirds of school were uncertain as to when to contact social services about their child protection concerns, with half of these reporting this to be a major concern. The timing and approach to referring a child protection case to social services can be crucial in ensuring that the child is successfully protected. Yet many teachers are concerned that passing on their observations and concerns may result in major disruptions to the lives of the child and family which may turn out to be unnecessary. This section explores the sensitive and often complex issues related to referring suspected abuse to social services.

## *Child Protection Liaison Teachers*

All teachers are supported in their role in child protection by a colleague who is designated as the Child Protection Liaison Teacher (CPLT). This colleague will usually have gained expertise in child protection through monitoring and advising on all cases in school, attending training and working with other agencies on child protection cases. Baginsky (2000) found that 92 per cent of CPLTs had received appropriate training, including initial training and higher-level joint training with other professionals.

The CPLT is the first person you should discuss your concerns with, even if you have not reached the stage of believing that a referral should be made to child protection services. If, after this discussion, you agree with the CPLT that further action should be taken, she should contact social services to do one of two things: seek further advice on how to proceed, or make a referral to child protection services.

However, you should consult with social services directly if you are unable to talk to the CPLT promptly or if your concerns persist despite discussion with the CPLT and she does not agree to take the matter further.

## *Making a child protection referral*

It is possible that after taking advice the CPLT makes a referral to social services; or social services decide to act on the information you have given.

Not all types of abuse require the same response. The options available include:

♦ child protection referral – if there is evidence of physical or sexual abuse then a referral to social services should be made promptly

♦ single agency response – if there are concerns about neglect or emotional abuse you may agree to monitor the situation and work with the parents on your concerns

♦ multi-agency response – you may agree to work with other agencies to provide support to the family.

A referral to social services should always be made in the following circumstances:

♦ where the child makes an allegation of abuse

♦ where there are physical injuries which are cause for concern

♦ where there are concerns about sexual abuse

♦ where there are concerns about emotional abuse or neglect and the situation has deteriorated to the extent that the child may be suffering significant harm

♦ where a child is being refused vital medical treatment

♦ where there is a credible allegation from a member of the public

♦ where the child is in contact with an individual who may put them at risk

♦ where there are further concerns about a child who is already on the Child Protection Register.

If a referral is to be made, several steps need to be taken first, usually by the CPLT in conjunction with senior staff. These are:

♦ the parents should be informed that a referral is to be made (unless this will put the child at significant further risk)

♦ the child's name should be checked against the Child Protection Register to see if he is listed

♦ other staff involved directly with the child should be asked to give any information they have which may contribute to knowledge of the child's situation and condition.

Your role at this stage is to ensure that the information you give is accurate and detailed. Referrals can be made in the following ways:

♦ completing an inter-agency referral form for reporting suspected child abuse to social services, which should be available in school

♦ making a telephone referral first in situations where there appears to be some urgency.

Either way it is important to record your concerns as soon as possible.

Information given should be considered carefully to ensure: it is accurate and detailed, based on observation; it is fact-based and not opinion, rumour or hearsay; the source of the information is clearly stated; and the language used is descriptive, not emotive.

The report should include:

♦ basic details about the child, e.g. name, age, address, class, any special needs or particular issues affecting the child, including any communication difficulties the child may have

♦ details of your concerns including dates and any discussion you have had with the child and parents about these concerns

♦ details of any discussions you have had with other staff about your concerns

♦ the level of your concern and how far you believe the child is at risk.

You can discuss the report with the CPLT to ensure that it is appropriately written and contains all necessary information.

## *Reasons not to report abuse?*

For many professionals, including teachers, reporting abuse is a momentous act, requiring careful consideration and generating much anxiety in the decision-making process. What if you are wrong and no abuse has taken place? What will happen to the family? What if they remove the child? What if you have made things worse for the child? What if there is a simple explanation for the injuries or indicators you have observed? What if the parents come to school and confront you?

Many professionals feel that reporting abuse could have highly negative consequences for the child and family, and possibly for the agency and individual practitioner as well.

Consider some of the reasons given for not reporting abuse:

- the child may experience further abuse

- the parents may suffer from unfounded allegations, possibly separation from their child and even criminal charges

- the child may be unnecessarily removed from the family

- the family may break down

- the individual who reports the abuse may be at risk from the child's parents

- the allegation may harm the reputation of the organization or agency

- the child abuse enquiry may cause stress to all involved

- there may be repercussions for all involved.

Despite these genuine concerns, it remains the responsibility of all professionals involved in working with children to ensure their safety from abuse. It is important to remember that the majority of children are not removed from the care of their families during a child protection enquiry and, of those who are, the majority only go into public care in the short-term. In respect of the other concerns, it is important that procedures are followed to minimize distress to all those involved and that parents are treated with respect and sensitivity and kept informed, in line with the principles of the Children Act 1989.

## *Confidentiality*

The process of referring a child who may be abused to social services will obviously involve a number of staff, including the CPLT and possibly the headteacher. It may involve discussions with other staff who have close contact with the child involved. It is vital that issues of confidentiality are clearly considered in any suspected child abuse case. The basic 'rule of thumb' is to avoid discussing the issues with anyone who does not 'need to know'. The minimum number of staff possible should be aware of the issues and all discussions should take place privately.

The school should have systems for confidential storage of written information about sensitive issues and you should make yourself aware of these. All written notes need to be kept safely away from others and only made available to the agreed staff directly involved with the situation. Finally, the process of being involved in a case of suspected abuse may be very stressful and distressing to you personally, as discussed later on in this book. Despite this, it is important not to discuss the details of the case or share sensitive information with family members or friends.

## *Working with parents*

The Children Act 1989, and *Working Together* both emphasize the need to include parents in the child protection process and to work in partnership with them to safeguard the child. Baginsky (2000) found that 92 per cent of schools had concerns about how to maintain a relationship with parents where child protection concerns had arisen. Parents may be very threatened by the process of discussing and responding to your concerns about their child. It is important to be aware of the procedures in your school for approaching parents about concerns and who is responsible for this. Parents need to be treated with respect and tact during the child protection investigation if their co-operation is to be secured.

Some keys issues to consider are:

♦ ensuring all discussions are private and confidential

♦ avoiding accusations or emotional responses to the situation

♦ ensuring that parents are listened to

♦ responding calmly to any anger or distress the parent may show

♦ avoiding threats of further action or displays of authority

♦ explaining clearly to parents what you intend to do next and who will be involved

♦ ensuring that parents who do not have English as a first language are supported in their communication, through an interpreter if necessary.

Parents may be very angry or defensive or extremely distressed by the child protection enquiry and this may give you concerns about your own safety (as discussed above in the section on 'Reasons not to report abuse?'). It is important to discuss any worries you have with the

CPLT and senior management and to pass on information about any threats or harassment you may receive.

## *Injured children*

In very rare circumstances, the child may be in school with injuries that require immediate attention. In this case, the child needs to be taken to hospital for immediate assessment and treatment and every effort should be made to contact the parents and involve them in this process. Hospital social work staff should be informed and the situation assessed after medical diagnosis and any treatment is given.

Figure 1: 'Responding to suspected child abuse in school' (see page 35) provides a quick guide to how to proceed where abuse is considered to have taken place.

## *The child protection enquiry*

The majority of reports of child abuse go to social services child protection services. However, in situations where it is clear that the child has been harmed by someone outside the family, it may be appropriate to refer to the police, who have specialist Child Protection Units to deal with such cases.

Local authorities have a duty to investigate any allegations of child abuse under Section 47 of the Children Act 1989. The main purposes of any such investigation are to establish the facts and make a record of them, to assess the risk to the child as a basis for taking action to protect him, and to assess the extent to which the child's needs are being met within the family.

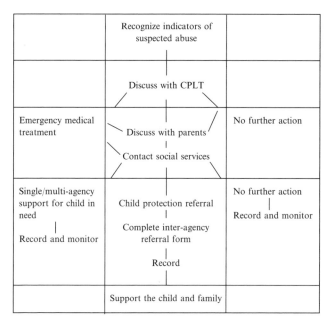

**Fig. 1.** Responding to suspected child abuse in school

Since 2000, assessment of the child and family, which is a central part of any investigation, is achieved through the *Framework for Assessment of Children in Need and their Families* (DoH, 2000), which is a detailed assessment tool used to establish the child's needs and the extent to which they are being met within the family and wider environment.

## Action following a child protection referral

There are a number of stages which the investigation must go through in order to achieve its goals. These are outlined in Figure 2: 'Child Protection Enquiries' on page 49 and listed in detail on the following pages.

1. Initial assessment within the *Framework for Assessment* by an experienced child protection social worker, within seven days from referral, covering:

   ♦ the needs of the child

   ♦ whether the parents can meet these needs, safeguard the child and promote her health and development

   ♦ whether action is required to safeguard and promote the child's welfare.

   The initial assessment will involve:

   ♦ the child

   ♦ the parents and any other significant adult

   ♦ other professionals involved with the child and family

   ♦ the referring professional/agency

   ♦ any written records relevant to the enquiry.

   The initial assessment will conclude whether:

   ♦ immediate action, possibly legal measures, should be taken to protect the child

   ♦ a child protection enquiry should be instigated under Section 47 of the Children Act 1989

   ♦ the child and her family should be referred for

family support services under Section 17 of the Children Act 1989, as a 'child in need'

♦ no further action should be taken.

A Section 47 enquiry will be instigated if it is decided on initial assessment that: the child is in need or there is reasonable cause to suspect that the child is suffering or likely to suffer significant harm.

2. To complete a Section 47 enquiry, assessment within the *Framework for Assessment* will take place to establish:

♦ the nature and extent of any harm or impairment to health and development the child may have suffered

♦ the extent to which parents can safeguard and promote the child's welfare and meet the child's needs

♦ other resources available to the child and family

♦ the extent of risk to the child

♦ whether immediate action is required to protect the child

♦ the type and range of services which may be required to support and protect the child and her family.

In order to complete this assessment, actions may include: taking the child for medical or other assessment; seeking the knowledge and views of other involved professionals; a strategy discussion with the police and other relevant professionals to plan how and what to do next; or searching existing records about the child.

3. If it is considered that there is a high level of risk of acute physical harm to the child, the social worker may:

   ♦ try and persuade the suspected abuser to leave the household or make other arrangements to safeguard the child in the short-term

   ♦ apply for an Emergency Protection Order (EPO)

   ♦ apply for a Child Assessment Order, if the parents refuse access to the child for medical or other assessment.

## The role of teaching staff in a Section 47 enquiry

Your role is outlined in the *Working Together to Safeguard Children* guidelines (DoH, 1999). In summary, it includes:

♦ having the knowledge and ability to recognize indicators of possible abuse

♦ making considered decisions, in conjunction with the CPLT, about referring children to social services where abuse is suspected

- ensuring that all communication with parents is sensitive, professional and non-judgemental

- making accurate and detailed referral reports based on observation

- ensuring that the investigating social worker is aware of any special needs or communication difficulties the child may have

- giving information to any social worker involved in a Section 47 enquiry

- supporting the child in school and being aware of the stress the enquiry may place on the child and his family

- maintaining confidentiality of speech and written records.

## The child protection case conference

The next stage of the child protection process is the child protection case conference. This meeting involves: professionals involved with the child and family; professionals who may offer a service to protect the child and/or support the family in the future; and the parents.

The child protection case conference is usually convened by the social services and chaired by a senior social services staff member or specially appointed professional.

## *Who attends child protection case conferences?*

Those involved can include:

♦ social worker and other social services staff

♦ health visitor, GP and any other relevant health professionals involved with the family, e.g. speech therapist, physiotherapists

♦ teaching staff, headteacher

♦ voluntary sector services staff, e.g. Home-Start, SureStart, NSPCC

♦ LEA staff, e.g. educational psychologist

♦ any other involved professionals

♦ parents

♦ interpreter if parents do not have English as their first language.

Parents may be invited to all or part of the child protection case conference, depending on the ACPC guidelines for the local authority.

## *What does the case conference do?*

The purpose of the child protection case conference is to:

♦ pool information about the child and any concerns about her

- discuss factors which affect the functioning of the family

- assess the risk of further abuse and the extent of concern about the child

- make plans to safeguard the child and support the family.

The child protection case conference makes two decisions: who is to be the key worker for the child (usually a social worker) and who will be in the 'core group' and whether the child's name should be added to the Child Protection Register.

## The Child Protection Register

The Child Protection Register is a centrally held record of children considered to be at risk of abuse. It is used to ensure that professionals can find out if a child has suffered previous abuse and there are ongoing concerns. Registration also triggers the commitment of resources to a child and family to safeguard the child and help the family to cope better, or remove the child to alternative carers. While a child's name is on the register, there will be ongoing review case conferences to monitor the child's welfare and situation.

## Child protection case conference recommendations

The child protection case conference also makes a series of recommendations designed to support and promote the child's welfare and the parents' ability to parent safely and effectively. These recommendations are incorporated in a child protection plan, which sets out goals for how involved agencies can contribute to safeguarding and promoting the child's welfare. The plan may include legal action to protect the child as discussed in the section on 'Legal and Procedural Issues'. This may involve, in a small number of cases, removal of the child into local authority care on a short- or long-term basis. If the child has already been removed from home on an EPO, the child protection case conference will agree whether the child should go home, or an Interim Care Order should be applied for, or other arrangements made to safeguard the child. The child protection plan is subject to regular review and is monitored by the key worker.

## Core groups

The 'core group' is made up of professionals with direct responsibility for the child and family. They monitor and discuss the progress of the child protection plan in between case conferences. You may be involved in the 'core group' for a particular child in your care. However, research evidence shows that 'core groups' often fade away after the initial case conference, leaving the social services to monitor and implement the child protection plan alone. Clearly, this is not in line with current guidelines and policy, and continuing efforts to strengthen multi-agency approaches to child protection are taking place, with more initiatives in the pipeline since the Victoria Climbie enquiry.

## *The role of teachers in the child protection case conference*

Your role includes:

♦ attending the case conference, depending on school policy

♦ writing a report to the case conference, outlining your involvement with the child and family, and grounds for concern about the child

♦ giving information about any special needs or communication difficulties the child may have

♦ discussing or adding to your report within the case conference

♦ answering any questions others may have within the case conference

♦ giving information clearly and accurately, in non-emotive, descriptive language

♦ contributing to the decisions and recommendations made within the case conference

♦ core group membership

♦ developing and implementing the child protection plan.

## The child protection plan

This plan is developed and implemented by the core group. Its targets include: ensuring the child's safety;

promoting his welfare; and supporting the family in parenting more safely and effectively.

It will also outline the roles of different agencies in implementing the plan. In a small number of cases, it may contain plans to remove the child from the parents' care.

The school may be asked to contribute to the child protection plan. This may involve:

♦ monitoring the child's attendance and absences

♦ monitoring the child's appearance and behaviour

♦ assessing and monitoring the child's educational progress

♦ supporting and promoting improvements in parenting through contact with the child's parents

♦ any other actions aimed at safeguarding and promoting the child's health and development

♦ reporting any concerns to the key worker.

You may be involved in supporting or co-ordinating other professional services that are delivered to the child within school, e.g. speech therapy, physiotherapy, and special needs services. Services provided and support given should take into account:

♦ the child's needs and any special needs

♦ the family's needs and any special needs

♦ the child and family's first language, culture and religion

- the child's and family's preferences in types of services

- cost, transport and accessibility of services.

## *Review child protection case conferences*

After the initial case conference, review dates will be set if the child's name is placed on the Child Protection Register. Reviews will:

1. Be held at six-monthly intervals or less

2. Be used to monitor the child's welfare

3. Assess the progress of implementing the child protection plan

4. Provide a forum for professionals and relevant others to raise concerns about the child

5. Amend the child protection plan as required

6. Deregister the child (take her name off the Child Protection Register) during a review case conference if:

   - the risk of abuse has decreased significantly for any reason

   - the child has left the area and another authority has responsibility

   - the child has reached 18, or has got married

   - the child has died.

Risk to the child may be reduced by improvements in parenting, the abuser leaving the household, the child leaving the household, or the child being in local authority care.

Once the child's name has been removed from the Child Protection Register, the child is no longer in the child protection system. However, the child may be deemed a 'child in need' and assessment and support may continue under Section 17 of the Children Act 1989, and within the *Framework for Assessment of Children in Need and their Families*.

This section is summarized in Figure 2: 'Child protection enquiries' on the next page.

## Checklist for action

Find out:

♦ who your school CPLT is

♦ where the inter-agency referral form for reporting suspected abuse to social services is and who is responsible for completing it

♦ what arrangements are in place for checking the Child Protection Register and who does this

♦ who goes to child protection case conferences from your school

♦ how confidential information about suspected child abuse is recorded and stored in your school and who is responsible for this

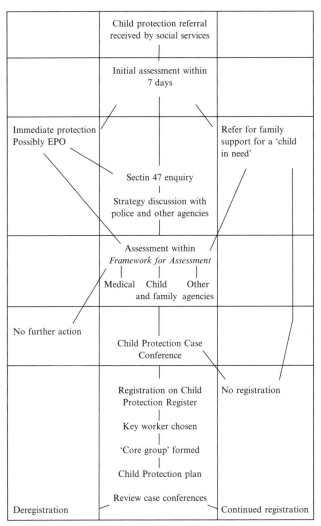

**Fig. 2.** Child protection enquiries

**3**

# Legal and procedural issues

## Introduction

Perhaps one of the most difficult areas of child protection is relating the legal framework, which determines and limits professional responses to suspected abuse, to the real lives and experiences of the children and families with whom you are in contact. The legal and procedural framework not only determines what is and is not perceived as abusive at any point in time, it also gives powers and duties to a range of professionals. You need to be aware of the responsibilities and the limits on the roles of other child protection professionals as well as your own role.

It can be very difficult, for example, to understand why social services do not remove some children from homes where they seem to be poorly parented. Your concerns about the child may be rooted in the quality of care the child receives, but the extent of the harm to the child may not be seen as significant enough to be described as abusive, within the legal definitions. This can be frustrating, especially where other professionals are involved. However, it may be that raising your concerns results in the child and family being assessed and receiving 'children in need' services instead of a child protection response. This can be very positive in supporting the family in parenting more effectively, and in improving the child's condition.

Knowledge and understanding of the legal process can help you to perform your role more effectively and improve relationships with other professionals through a clearer understanding of the requirements and limitations of their role. This section looks at the legal and procedural basis for child protection and supporting 'children in need', the role of different professionals within this and, specifically, the role of teaching staff and schools.

# The Children Act 1989

Part V of the Children Act 1989 incorporates the legal basis for child protection by statutory agencies in England and Wales. The Act is based on a number of key principles which created the ethos in which child protection work should take place. These principles are essentially child-centred, emphasizing that the child is a central part of the process, not an object to be acted upon. They also emphasize the role of 'partnership' and 'working together', between families and professionals and between professionals from different agencies, as key factors in providing good quality child protection services.

## *Key principles of the Children Act 1989*

♦ The child's welfare is paramount.

♦ Delay in legal processes is prejudicial to the child's welfare and should be avoided.

♦ Courts should only make orders where it is better for the child to do so than not (the non-interventionist principle).

♦ Decisions should be made in partnership between professionals from different agencies and families.

♦ The child's views and opinions should be considered (but cannot override the need for the child's welfare to be paramount).

♦ 'Parental responsibility' is retained by parents throughout, even if the child is in care (it is transferred only through the making of an adoption order).

## *Section 47*

This is the section of the Children Act 1989 under which local authorities have a duty to investigate suspected child abuse cases and take steps to ensure the child's welfare is safeguarded.

This duty is normally taken up through local authority social services departments. Education and health authorities are given a duty to support and assist Section 47 investigations. This means that as teachers you:

♦ may be called on to provide information about a child's welfare or behaviour, any special needs or communication difficulties

♦ may be asked to relate any incidents involving the child or concerns you may have about him

♦ may need to discuss the child's educational progress and any problems with this.

Determining whether intervention should take place
or not is a key issue within such an investigation. What
is the benchmark for deciding whether a child is abused
or at risk of abuse? The concept of 'significant harm'
plays a key role in this decision.

## *'Significant harm'*

This term is used to describe the threshold for legally
based intervention in a case of suspected abuse. The
child must be deemed to be suffering, or likely to
suffer, significant harm for such intervention to take
place. 'Harm' is defined as:

> *ill-treatment or the impairment of health and devel-*
> *opment.*
>
> (Section 31, Children Act 1989).

'Development' refers to all aspects of the child's
physical, emotional and social development and learning development. In effect, it is not sufficient for the
local authority or any professional involved with the
child to believe that the child is not being adequately
parented. There must be evidence that the quality of
parenting will result in or has resulted in 'significant
harm' to the child. This is now ascertained through a
comprehensive assessment of the child and her family
within the *Framework of Assessment of Children in
Need and their Families* (DoH, 2000) (see page 60).

This assessment determines whether the child is suffering significant harm and whether child protection services should become involved. Teaching staff must ensure that they keep records of their concerns about any child as these may be part of the assessment process and contribute to determining whether a child is suffering significant harm. During a child protection investigation, child protection social workers and experienced medical staff will be involved in assessing the extent of any harm to the child.

## Court orders under the Children Act 1989

There are a number of legal orders that the court can make which are used in child protection cases to safeguard the welfare of the child. The non-interventionist principle mentioned above emphasizes that court orders should only be made if this will improve the child's situation. This means that the court can make a positive decision not to make any order if this best safeguards the child's welfare. The court also has a right to decide to make a different order to the one that is applied for. Court orders are normally applied for by local authorities in the shape of social services, but the NSPCC and the police can also apply for some orders, as can the LEA in some situations. Court orders will be granted if it is in a child's best interests for the court to make the order. Evidence presented to the court can be drawn from the range of professionals involved with the child, so it is important that your records of any incident are clear and comprehensive.

## *Emergency Protection Orders*

An EPO is used to remove the child to, or keep the child in, a safe place when the child is considered to be in 'acute physical danger'. It is used where:

♦ delay could be extremely harmful to the child and immediate action to protect the child needs to be taken

♦ when a child protection investigation is taking place and access to the child is being 'unreasonably refused'.

The person applying for the EPO must ensure that no alternative arrangements can be made to safeguard the child, such as:

♦ parents agreeing to the child being accommodated (cared for by the local authority)

♦ parents agreeing that the child can placed with a suitable relative or other person

♦ the person suspected of abuse agreeing to leave the household for the time being.

If a child at your school is removed from home on an EPO, every effort should be made to ensure that his schooling is not disrupted. However, in reality a child could be placed far from home and arrangements to get him to and from school may take some time to arrange.

EPO's are short term, lasting eight days initially, with provision for a seven-day extension. After this time, the child must:

♦ be made subject to an Interim Care Order (see below);

♦ allowed to return home;

♦ other arrangements must made for the child to stay with a suitable person; or

♦ the child must be accommodated by the local authority with the parents' agreement.


## Child Assessment Orders

Child Assessment Orders were a new provision within the Children Act 1989, in response to child death inquiries such as that of Kimberley Carlile (DHSS, 1987), which highlighted the need for a legal basis for ensuring that a child's health and welfare can be assessed when parents are not co-operative. The CAO is used to ensure that local authority social services can gain access to a child for medical or other type of assessment.

Criteria for successfully applying for a CAO include proving:

♦ that the child may suffer or be likely to suffer from significant harm;

♦ that an assessment is necessary to determine this; and

♦ that an assessment is unlikely to take place without the CAO.

A CAO lasts for seven days and requires the parents to make the child available for specific assessments, which could include stays away from home. Assessment is interpreted very broadly and can include: physical assessment; mental health assessment; psychological assessment; educational assessment; or any other relevant assessment, such as sight and hearing.

Schools may be involved in educational assessments as part of this process. However, children who have 'sufficient understanding to make an informed decision' can refuse an assessment.

## Care Orders

A Care Order made in respect of any child results in that child being placed in the care of the local authority, although the parents continue to share parental responsibility. The child must be shown to be suffering from or likely to suffer from significant harm; and this must be due to the standard of care she receives; or because the child is beyond parental control.

The child is 'looked after' by the local authority until the Care Order expires (when the child is 18) or is revoked, usually through application by the parents. Making a Care Order involves the long-term removal of the child from the parents' care, and as such, is a very serious step for a court to take. Prior to taking such a step the applicant (normally local authority social services, although the NSPCC can apply) must:

♦ make rigorous efforts to help the parents to parent more safely and effectively; and

♦ ensure that extensive consultation with all involved agencies, the parents and, where possible, the child has taken place.

The court can make an Interim Care Order for eight weeks to give the local authority time to make a full case, for example, where an EPO has previously been made and it is not considered safe for the child to go back to his parents' care.

While the Care Order is in place, the local authority has to promote contact between the child and her significant others, except where there is considerable risk, in which case an application can be made to deny contact with named individuals.

There are a number of options for the care of a child on a Care Order. When placing a child 'looked after', local authorities normally try to:

♦ place all children under 12 with foster parents rather than in residential care, although this option is usually open for older children

♦ meet the child's needs in terms of religion, culture and language

♦ take into consideration such factors as ease of contact with significant others and continuity in schooling or nursery.

However, in most local authorities there is a significant shortage of the full range of foster carers required. Lack of suitable placements can result in additional disruption to the child's life, and placements may be a long way from the child's familiar environment. Shortages of appropriate foster placements particularly affect older children, children with disabilities and children from non-white families.

## *Personal Education Plans*

Schools have specific responsibilities towards children 'looked after' by the local authority. Each child in public care must have a Personal Education Plan (PEP) which is regularly reviewed. The plan contains targets and focuses on the child's individual educational needs.

It has been established that children who are in public care:

♦ often have disrupted schooling

♦ may often have missed out on early years' education and support in their pre-school learning

♦ may have moved between placements on a number of occasions, attending a series of different schools

♦ have poorer levels of achievement and educational progress than average

♦ have poorer outcomes in terms of qualifications and progression to further and higher education than average

♦ may have social and emotional problems which affect progress in school.

Educational outcomes for children 'looked after' were identified as a major problem in the Utting Report, *People Like Us* (DoH, 1997). Since the recommendations of this report were implemented, there has been much more rigorous tracking of the educational progress of children 'looked after' and more support to meet their educational needs. Each school now has a designated teacher for children 'looked after' (often the same staff member as the Child Protection Liaison Teacher), who has responsibility for monitoring and supporting the education of children in care. Many children in care struggle with issues of low self-esteem and poor self-confidence, and may find it hard to make friends and join in activities in school.

In terms of children 'looked after' in school, teaching staff may be involved in implementing and reviewing PEPs, providing emotional and social support, providing learning support, and referring children to other agencies for additional support or help.

## Supervision Orders

Supervision Orders can be made from one to three years. They allow the local authority to monitor and support the child and family where there are concerns about the child's welfare but no immediate need to remove the child from the parents' care. The child is usually supervised by a social worker who is charged with advising, assisting and befriending her and ensuring the parents co-operate with the supervisory process.

## Accommodated children

In some cases, where there are significant difficulties for the parents in continuing to care at a particular point in time, the family may agree with social services that the child should be accommodated by the local authority. This agreement is made on a voluntary basis, and although the child will be 'looked after' by the local authority, there is no legal basis for keeping the child in care once the parents wish to resume their role. The parents can reclaim their child at any time. Children are sometimes accommodated as an alternative to a court order, where there is a high level of agreement between parents and the social services. Accommodation can be a long- or short-term arrangement.

## Section 17, 'children in need'

Within the Children Act 1989 there is provision for local authorities to safeguard and promote the welfare of 'children in need' in order to prevent them from suffering harm or neglect and to reduce the numbers of children on care and supervision orders in the area.

'Children in need' are defined as those who require local authority services in order to:

♦ achieve 'a reasonable standard of health and development';

♦ to avoid significant impairment to their health and development; or

♦ are children with disabilities.

Since 2000 there has been a common assessment framework (see *Framework for Assessment of Children in Need and their Families*, pages 62–3) for all children and families where abuse is suspected or the child is considered to be in need. This common assessment framework was introduced to provide a more comprehensive and standard response to all children in need and to ensure that assessment led effectively to the provision of appropriate services. It is also aimed at bridging the gap between child protection and family support services so that children and families can more easily access services from both at different times as required.

## *Working Together to Safeguard Children*

One of the key procedural documents you need to be aware of is the Department of Health guidelines, *Working Together to Safeguard Children* (DoH, 1999), which provide every relevant professional with information about their role in child protection. The guidelines also include definitions of abuse (see pages 5–19) and information about the indicators of abuse. They give clear instructions to different groups of professionals about their responsibilities in the child protection process. The guidelines are very readable and can be useful in helping to clarify issues about abuse of which you are unsure. They can be found at www.doh.gov.uk.

The guidelines are periodically updated as new procedures are developed. Their main message is the need for different agencies to work together more effectively to protect children. In the 1980s, in particular, a stream of child death inquiry reports concluded that failures in co-operation and communication between relevant agencies were significant in contributing to circumstances that led to the child's death (DHSS, 1985). The need for different agencies involved with children to overcome professional barriers and work better together continues to be a key issue in developing better practice in child protection.

# Area Child Protection Committees (ACPCs)

The *Working Together* guidelines are used as a basis for developing local child protection procedures, currently produced by multi-agency Area Child Protection Committees (ACPCs). The ACPC is made up of senior representatives from agencies involved with children within the local authority, including health, social services, education, probation, and voluntary sector organizations.

They are responsible for:

♦ establishing and monitoring child protection procedures

♦ promoting and resourcing a multi-agency approach to child protection

♦ child protection training

♦ reviewing particular cases, e.g. where a child has died

♦ producing an annual report on child protection in the area.

A copy of the ACPC child protection procedures for the area should be available in all schools and staff should have access to it. *Working Together* is discussed more fully in the section on 'Working Together: a multi-agency approach to child protection', pages 64–80.

## *Framework for Assessment of Children in Need and their Families*

The *Framework for Assessment of Children in Need and their Families* (DoH, 2000) is a set of guidelines for assessing children and families to determine whether the child and family require services for 'children in need', whether a child protection investigation should take place, and the specific needs of the child and family.

The concept of a comprehensive assessment framework is important in ensuring that children and their families receive the right services to meet their needs. Children are assessed within this framework whether abuse is suspected or not. It may be important that some children and families receive services for 'children in need' under Section 17 of the Children Act 1989, as well as child protection services, to provide support that may prevent further abuse taking place. According to *Working Together to Safeguard Children* (DoH, 1999: 2.27) the framework embraces three key areas: the child's developmental needs; the parents' capacity to meet these needs; and wider family and environmental factors.

Although social services take a lead role in any assessment of a child and family, it is clear that other agencies are required to offer information, expertise and support towards the assessment and provision of services to the child and family. Schools may be involved in assessment of:

♦ the child's educational achievements and ability

♦ the child's behaviour and any difficulties in school

♦ the child's ability to access the curriculum

♦ the parent/child relationship

♦ the parent's ability and willingness to support the child in school.

The impact of the introduction of the *Assessment Framework* on the roles and responsibilities of relevant professionals is discussed more fully in the section on 'Working Together: a multi-agency approach to child protection', pages 64–80.

## Checklist for action

♦ Locate the key government documents, *Working Together to Safeguard Children* and the *Framework for Assessment* (www.doh.gov.uk).

♦ Check your responsibilities as outlined in the Area Child Protection Procedures and any school procedures available.

♦ Read the DfES guidelines on supporting children 'looked after' in schools (www.dfes.gov.uk).

**4**

# Working together: a multi-agency approach to child protection

## Introduction

One of the key features of the current child protection system is the emphasis on 'working together' and a multi-agency approach to protecting children from abuse. Evidence from a series of child death inquiry reports and research into the child protection process supports the widely-held view that child protection works best when the different agencies and professionals involved are working in close co-operation and harmony with each other. The principles underpinning this approach are made clear in *Working Together to Safeguard Children* (DoH, 1999), the Children Act 1989 and other key documents on child protection. Clearly there is a need for agencies to work in close co-operation to support children and families where abuse has taken place. Efforts to achieve successful multi-agency approaches to child protection have come a long way in recent years, but there remain a number of difficulties with 'working together'.

Professionals working in the child protection system are drawn from a range of agencies with different objectives, ethoses, legal and procedural boundaries, and professional training and qualifications. There may be misconceptions or suspicions between agencies, and groups of practitioners may hold well-established stereotypes about other professionals. Even the differences in jargon used by professionals can create barriers to effective communication and the development of co-operative relationships. There are a number of initiatives to improve working relationships between professionals in child protection, including joint training provided by ACPCs. However, this type of training is not available to all staff and may not be resourced adequately in all authorities.

Teachers have a significant role to play in child protection, yet there is evidence that many are confused about this role and lack confidence in dealing with child protection cases. Identifying abuse and making decisions about whether to refer cases to social services are key areas where teaching staff may feel ill-equipped to cope.

In this section, we will explore the roles of different professionals within the child protection process and discuss the ways in which 'working together' can be successfully promoted.

## Professional roles in child protection

### *Social workers*

The majority of child protection social workers work in local authority social services departments. However, a significant number may be employed by children's charities such as the NSPCC, Barnardos and NCH. The NSPCC is the only charitable body to have legal responsibilities within the Children Act 1989, reflecting a long history of pioneering work in the field of child protection.

Social workers have lead responsibility within the child protection process, within legal and procedural boundaries. Social workers are supervised by senior staff and social services usually have specialist child protection officers to offer advice and support to other social workers. Some social workers are based in hospitals, supporting children and families, pregnant women, and families where adult drug abuse or substance abuse may be seen as possibly harmful to children.

Under Section 47 of the Children Act 1989, social services have a duty to investigate suspected child abuse. Social workers involved in this process are expected to work with other professionals and agencies to achieve this, and to involve parents in the process as much as is possible. Their main tasks are to:

♦ receive and respond to referrals from other agencies and members of the public

♦ check if the child is on the Child Protection Register

♦ take steps to protect the child immediately if the child is at risk of 'acute physical harm'

♦ gather information about the child and family directly and from other significant professionals

♦ assess the family within the *Framework for Assessment of Children in Need and their Families* (DoH, 2000)

- convene a child protection case conference as required, or

- refer the child for 'children in need' services

- take the role of key worker

- work with the core group to develop and implement the child protection plan

- ensure that the child's welfare and safety are monitored and reviewed

- propose the removal of the child's name from the Child Protection Register as appropriate.

The role of the social worker is complex and demanding, requiring them to investigate possible child abuse within the family while developing a relationship with the child and family and assessing their needs for family support services. Social services main remit is to protect the child and promote her welfare, possibly through working with parents to improve parenting standards and safety for the child within the home. In performing this task, they must take into account the child and family's linguistic, religious and cultural needs.

## *Police*

The police have a duty to investigate crime and as such they are involved in child protection cases where it seems likely that a crime against a child has taken place. These are most likely to be cases where there is evidence of assault on the child or sexual abuse.

However, cases can be prosecuted where neglect or emotional abuse has taken place.

Police investigations are usually carried out by Police Child Protection Units staffed by experienced and specially trained officers. To promote better relationships between the police and social workers involved in child protection, there has been a marked increase in joint training and the development of closer working patterns in recent years. The strategy meeting which takes place early on in the child protection enquiry will determine the extent of police involvement and how the enquiry will be structured. Normally, social workers and the police will conduct joint investigations, including joint interviewing, to reduce stress on the child and family. However, there are fundamental differences in remit between the two agencies. While the police have a remit to investigate and apprehend offenders, social services have a duty to protect children from abuse. The main tasks of the police are:

♦ to investigate crimes against children

♦ to present evidence to the Crown Prosecution Service where such evidence indicates that an individual has committed such a crime

♦ to work jointly with social services and other agencies to protect children

♦ to safeguard the welfare of any child, including taking care and control of the child for up to 72 hours where the child is suffering acute harm.

With reference to the last point, the police have a legal duty to protect children under Section 26 of the Children Act 1989. Police powers include a duty to remove a child at risk of significant harm to a safe accommodation or to prevent a child being removed from safe accommodation, e.g. a hospital. Normally, the police involve the social services, but they can act independently.

## Health services

GPs have a responsibility to monitor the welfare of children in their care and to refer any concerns to social services. Health visitors have particular responsibilities towards children under five and are often the main professional involved with pre-school children. Health visitors are trained and many are experienced in determining possible indicators of abuse. Their role in monitoring the growth and development of young children is significant in recognizing the possibility of neglect or emotional abuse in children under five. The health visitor may also be the key professional involved in monitoring the welfare of young children and supporting families where abuse has taken place.

Children may be medically examined as part of assessment where abuse is suspected. Examinations are usually carried out by experienced paediatricians, often at a local hospital accident and emergency unit. The outcomes of such medical examinations may be crucial in determining whether abuse has taken place or not. However, abuse may come to light when children are in hospital for other reasons and therefore any medical staff may be involved in recognizing and reporting suspected abuse. The main tasks of health-care staff are:

♦ to promote the welfare of all children

♦ to monitor children's growth and development and record concerns

♦ to recognize and respond to any indicators of abuse

♦ to examine children for injuries, problems with growth and development, and emotional difficulties, where there are causes for concern

♦ to work with social services to determine whether a child has suffered 'significant harm'

♦ to support children and families where abuse has taken place, within the child protection plan.

## *Early years practitioners*

Nursery nurses, child-minders, out of school and crèche workers, and other practitioners working with young children, have a central role in the care and protection of young children. All centres for young children are now required to be aware of the possibility of abuse and to take steps to ensure that the children in their care are protected. Training and development for early years practitioners has become more consistently available recently, through the Early Years Development and Childcare Partnerships, and as such more workers are getting child protection training. Centres are required to develop their own child protection policies, and the EYDCPs have been instrumental in promoting and supporting higher levels of awareness, particularly among the independent and voluntary sectors.

Early years workers may also have a significant role in supporting families and children where abuse has taken place and monitoring the progress of children in their care. Their main tasks are:

♦ to support the welfare and development of all children in their care

♦ to recognize and respond to any indicators of abuse

♦ to refer concerns to social services as necessary

♦ to work with social services and other agencies to safeguard children where abuse may have taken place

♦ to support children and families where abuse has taken place and to monitor children's welfare within child protection plans.

## Voluntary and charitable organizations

There are many other local and national organizations which work to support children and families where children are at risk or have been abused. Barnardos, NCH and the NSPCC all run projects to support children in different ways, according to local needs. These projects include family centres, home visiting services and support services for children who have been abused. There are innumerable local charities who perform similar functions. Increasingly, these agencies have taken over many of the family support services formerly offered by local authorities. Many services, such as family centres, are jointly funded by charitable and voluntary sector agencies, local authority social services, health and education. Other national organizations contributing to child protection are Childline, a telephone advice and referral service, and Home-Start, a home visiting service linking parent volunteers with families in needs.

SureStart projects, funded through central government, have become central to the organization and development of family support services for families of children under four. They establish and develop community-based health and social services, drawing in local authority and NHS services as well as independent, charitable and voluntary sector provision within the SureStart area. Their main remit is to improve educational and health standards for pre-school children, but they also have a mandate to develop child protection services and support children at risk within the communities where they are based.

The role of voluntary sector agencies varies but includes supporting and promoting children's welfare, recognizing and responding to any indicators of abuse, referring suspected abuse to social services, and contributing to child protection plans and monitoring the welfare of children.

## *Education*

Teachers have an important role in the support and protection of school-age children, resulting in a high percentage of child protection referrals coming through schools. School staff are uniquely placed to detect the indicators of abuse in the children in their care and to monitor progress and support children where abuse has taken place. All schools have a responsibility to designate a Child Protection Liaison Teacher who takes a lead role in developing child protection systems within the school. Teaching staff should have access to the ACPC Child Protection Procedures, LEA procedures and the school's own child protection procedures. However, many teachers do not feel adequately trained and able to respond effectively to suspected child abuse. Baginsky (2000: 4) found that:

*schools wanted all teachers to receive regular training in recognising the signs of abuse in children as well as in how to respond to suspicions and disclosures. Alongside this were calls for particular attention to be paid to students on teaching practice placements and newly qualified teachers within structured induction programmes.*

There is a lack of adequate training in child protection on many initial teacher training courses, a fact which has been highlighted by the Victoria Climbie inquiry. Despite the fact that child protection is part of the ITT curriculum, there is evidence that it is not given the same status or emphasis as academic subjects. A small survey in 1997 concluded that:

♦ not all ITT had a child protection element

♦ there are large variations in the amount of time given to child protection within the curriculum

♦ 'training in relation to child protection was extremely patchy' (Baginsky, 2000).

Not all teaching staff have access to training after qualification, and joint training with other professionals may only be available to a few. The author frequently asks students on placement in schools if they are given access to child protection procedures and advice on how to respond to suspected abuse, and finds that the average number of students who are given this information is usually around two in a group of 25–30. This is despite findings by Baginsky (2000) that 94 per cent of schools have a child protection policy in place.

The main tasks of teaching staff are:

♦ to promote the welfare of all children in their care

♦ to recognize and respond to any indicators of abuse

♦ to contribute observations and information to child protection investigations

♦ to monitor and support children where abuse has taken place, within the child protection plan.

Non-teaching staff also have a role in protecting children within schools. School health staff, in particular, have responsibility for monitoring the health and welfare of children in the schools they visit and for sharing their concerns with the CPLT if necessary.

## *Governors*

Normally, one governor is designated to deal with child protection issues within the school. Governors have a responsibility to monitor child protection in schools, including ensuring there is a child protection policy in place and responding to allegations of abuse against the headteacher.

## *LEAs*

The LEA has a role in providing advice and support on child protection issues to heads and teaching staff. How this is offered varies between different authorities, some having dedicated child protection officers, while others offer support through other services within the LEA. LEAs are represented on the ACPC and have a role in developing and monitoring child protection procedures in schools. Some LEAs draw up their own child protection procedures aimed at schools, whilst others distribute ACPC guidelines.

One of the most significant roles for LEAs in child protection is training, with the majority offering at least basic training for teachers. However, there are large variations in the amount and type of training offered, with some authorities 'buying in' training and others using social services trainers. The extent to which LEAs ensure all schools access child protection training also varies considerably. Baginsky (2000: 6) found that 10 per cent of schools had fewer than 25 per cent of their schools represented on training within a three-year period. The main tasks of the LEA are to provide written child protection procedures to schools, advice and support where child protection issues arise, and child protection training to school staff.

## *Working Together to Safeguard Children* (DoH, 1999)

The arrangements for inter-agency co-operation in child protection are outlined in the Department of Health guidelines, as discussed briefly in the section on 'Legal and Procedural Issues' (pages 48–63). These guidelines expand on the principles and provisions of the Children Act 1989, emphasizing partnership with parents and a multi-agency approach as the most effective way of protecting children. Schools have the following responsibilities within the guidelines (all the section references are from *Working Together to Safeguard Children*):

♦ general responsibility for the pastoral care of children (3.10)

♦ responsibility to ensure that policies and procedures are in place for the protection of children (3.10)

♦ ensuring that school is a safe environment (3.10)

♦ using the curriculum to promote child safety and make children aware of unacceptable behaviour towards them (3.10)

♦ recognizing and responding to indicators of abuse (3.11)

- ensuring that an enquiry is aware of a child's special needs or communication difficulties (3.11)

- referring child protection concerns and providing information to Section 47 (child protection) enquiries (3.12)

- working with social services and other agencies to develop and implement child protection plans (3.13).

## The teacher's role in working together

With reference to the points made above, your responsibilities can be varied and demanding. Some of these relate mainly to situations where a child protection issue has arisen. These have been discussed already in the section on 'Responding to suspected child abuse' (pages 25–47). Others relate to the ongoing whole-school development of a non-abusive environment for the children. These will be dealt with in the section on 'A whole-school approach to protecting children' (pages 96–100). In this section, your responsibilities to work together with other professionals will be discussed.

Teachers are increasingly working as part of multi-disciplinary teams in all aspects of their work, for example:

- in the classroom

- through special needs reviews

- through ongoing work with children with learning difficulties

♦ when working with children with English as a second language

♦ when working with children who may be in need or have been abused.

Any class may involve a range of adults involved in supporting the children, as well as the teacher. The author counted two parent volunteers, a childcare assistant supporting an individual pupil, an ESL support teacher and a nursery nurse student on placement, as well as the teacher, in one Y2 lesson. Yet despite this growing wealth of experience in teamwork, research evidence shows that there are often problems and misunderstandings and sometimes lack of co-operation when professionals work together in child protection. Key problem areas are differences in aims and objectives, approaches to work and work ethos, training and professional qualifications, pay and status, and use of language and different jargon.

For example, a child protection social worker has the key role in investigating abuse and protecting the child. While also having a role in protecting the child, a police officer has the key role in identifying, investigating and presenting evidence about any crime committed. A teacher has a role in child protection, but also has the education and welfare of 30 or more other children, the status of the school, relationships with parents and the community, and delivery of the curriculum to consider. All are trained differently, work different hours, have different pay and conditions and speak in different professional 'languages'. The requirement to work together across these differences can result in stress in those concerned, which may lead to the development of negative views of the other professional groups involved. These negative views may eventually develop into firmly held negative stereotypes which can then exert an influence on future inter-agency work. If professional differences become problematic the result can be poor communication, lack of inter-agency co-operation, unco-ordinated efforts to protect the child and support the family, failure to pass on key information and higher risk to the child and failure to support the family.

In order to combat the difficulties that can interfere with effective inter-agency work, there have been a number of strategies to try and improve understanding and co-operation between professionals from the range of disciplines. The key strategies to develop working together in child protection are:

♦ detailed procedures outlining the different professional roles and responsibilities

♦ the development of multi-agency Area Child Protection Committees (ACPCs)

♦ inter-agency protocols outlining how agencies will respond to each other in child protection situations

♦ joint training between professionals involved in protecting children.

In terms of individual teaching staff, there are a number of issues to consider in order to improve relationships with professionals from other agencies. These include:

♦ examining stereotypes and negative attitudes towards other professionals

♦ being prepared to ask for information and clarification as necessary

♦ becoming more aware of other agencies and professional roles in the child protection process

♦ being willing to share information, concerns and your experiences with other professionals

♦ accessing joint training where available.

# Checklist for action

♦ Check *Working Together* to clarify the roles of other professionals in child protection.

♦ Ask about the availability of joint child protection training within your authority.

♦ Check school child protection procedures for information on how you are expected to respond to other involved agencies.

♦ Check the ACPC procedures for inter-agency arrangements for co-operation in child protection cases.

♦ Talk to professionals from other agencies about their roles in child protection and any issues or concerns they may have about these.

**5**

# Working with children who may have been abused

## Introduction

The child protection process aims to safeguard children from abuse or further abuse and to ensure that their needs are adequately met. However, within this process the child may suffer distress and trauma resulting from both the abuse and the child protection process. Removal from the care of parents, however temporary, can be very upsetting to children, even when parents are abusive. Evidence shows that the majority of abused children want to stay with their parents, but want the abuse to stop. Many abused children will conceal their injuries or distress rather than risk being parted from their family. Not only do abused children often have attachments to their parents, but there are also often strong sibling attachments within the family which may be strained or disrupted in the child protection process.

Even if children are not removed from their parents' care, the child protection process can cause distress. The child may experience medical and other examinations and assessments. She may be asked to talk about difficult and distressing parts of her family life with strangers. She may be asked to describe traumatic events which have occurred within the family. She may feel that she is betraying her parents and other family members. Very young children may simply not know what is happening, but may be aware of tension, anxiety and distress in other family members. In cases where the abuser is prosecuted or has to leave the family home, the child may suffer acute guilt that she has been responsible for the family breakdown. In some cases the child's version of events may not be believed by family members, and it may be the child who feels outcast from the family home.

The child protection process is geared to trying to minimize the distress and trauma children and families may experience within the procedures. Interviewing children is handled by experienced social workers and police, and kept to the minimum. Children are often videoed giving evidence so that they do not have to do this in court in front of their alleged abuser. In all cases, keeping the family together if possible, or in contact, is a priority of the professionals involved. However, practical issues may cause problems. Children may be separated from each other if they are placed in foster homes. Contact with parents may be difficult if the children are placed some distance away. In this section, the ways in which you can support children and families where abuse has taken place will be discussed.

## The effects of abuse on the child

Children may be affected by abuse in many different ways. How the child responds in this situation can depend on many factors such as:

## Working with children who may have been abused

- the age and understanding of the child

- the child's character and personality

- the type and extent of the abuse

- the relationship between the child and the abuser

- the degree of support the child gets from other family members

- the standard of care the child receives within the home

- the extent to which the child's routines are disrupted

- the responses of the professionals involved.

Every child will respond uniquely to the effects of abuse. Some children may suffer lifelong problems and others may appear to be much less affected. The impact of abuse can be short or long-term. Some of the possible effects of abuse are:

- regressive behaviour, distress, sleeplessness, crying

- anger, aggression, withdrawal, unhappiness, fear

- lack of self-esteem, low self-confidence, unwillingness to tackle new tasks or experiences

- physical impairment

- sexualized behaviour towards adults or other children

- wetting, soiling, tantrums and outbursts

- obsessive or compulsive behaviour, e.g. self-mutilation, pulling out hair, ritualistic behaviour

- over-compliant behaviour, ingratiating towards adults, superficial relationships

- social and learning problems in school

- short- or long-term impairment to any or all aspects of growth and development.

This list is not definitive and children may express their distress in a myriad of different ways. In the long-term, where abuse has had a significant impact on the child and there has been a lack of supportive intervention, abused children may become adults who suffer: low self-esteem, and poor self-image; mental health problems, e.g. depression; alcohol and drug abuse problems; inability to make satisfactory relationships with others; abusive relationships; low educational attainment; and poor employment chances.

The child may feel overwhelmed by the events that have taken place, and may feel as if he cannot recover from the experiences he has had. This may result in depression or recklessness, as if the child simply does not care what happens to him, and truanting, aggression, sexually promiscuous behaviour and drug and alcohol misuse in older children.

However, there are strategies to support children through the child protection process and the aftermath of abuse which can ameliorate some of the effects of abuse and help the child to make sense of what has happened to her. Perhaps the best help a child can receive is the consistent support of familiar adults.

However, you may deal both with children who have been abused who are known to you, and children who have moved into the area and started at your school because abuse has lead to a change in their living situation.

## Dealing with the effects of abuse

An abused child may have a range of feelings about what has happened to her, and these may be conflicting and confused. Working through these feelings is the first step in coming to terms with the child's experiences. Sometimes these feelings lead to unwanted behaviour, or they may negatively influence the child's ability to socialize, learn and develop. Every child has her own reaction to abuse, but some of the common feelings include:

♦ anger towards the abuser and other adults who may have 'failed' to prevent the abuse

♦ guilt and shame, feeling responsible for the abuse taking place

♦ guilt about the possibility or actuality of family breakdown or the removal of the abuser from the home

♦ anxiety and fear about the future

♦ feelings of being unwanted, unloved, even hated by family members

♦ grief and loss at separation from parents, siblings and other significant people

- feeling out of control, helpless

- despair, depression, sadness.

Not every child will feel some or all of these types of feelings, but these have been found to be common in abused children. Some children who have been abused will receive therapeutic support to help them to overcome the negative effects of abuse. Types of supportive intervention could include: play therapy; art therapy; groupwork with other abused children; counselling support; psychotherapeutic support; family therapy; and support from a child psychologist.

Not all children will need this type of support or have access to it. There is evidence that some children would benefit from intervention where it is not available or affordable.

## The teacher's role in supporting the abused child

Teachers may have more contact with school-aged children who have been abused than any other professional involved. However, other demands on your time and energy may make it difficult to consider how you could best support a child in this situation. Research shows that changes in the teacher's roles and responsibilities in recent years may have reduced the time free to spend with individual children. These include:

- new curriculum demands and initiatives

- increases in recording and paperwork in general

- large classes

♦ more demanding timetables

♦ additional responsibilities for individual teachers.

Despite the limits on your time there are a number of ways in which you can support a child who has been abused.

## *Helping the child deal with feelings*

Perhaps one of the most difficult tasks you may have is understanding how the child may be feeling and helping her to come to terms with her distress, sadness, anger, guilt and a whole range of other responses she may have to the abuse. As discussed above, some children may receive specific support to help with this aspect, others may not. Whether the child is receiving therapeutic support or not, you are still probably spending more time with the child than any other professional and your role is significant. Some children find that school is a 'safe haven' in a world gone mad around them, and they may be grateful for the respite school provides from thinking about and responding to the upheavals they have gone through. Other children find it hard to go to school if there is uncertainty at home or there have been changes in the family situation. They may fear further changes in their absence and want to stay close to family members.

Supporting a child in this situation requires patience, tact and sensitivity. Some ways in which you can be supportive are:

- ensuring that the child has opportunity to share feelings without pressurizing him to talk

- giving the child 'time out' if he is becoming distressed or angry

- remaining consistent and positive

- offering the child the opportunity to do small tasks at breaks if he cannot face the playground

- pairing or grouping the child with mature, supportive children

- being sensitive to the effects of choices of materials, e.g. books which may reflect loss and sadness

- sharing concerns with parents or carers.

## *Difficult behaviour*

Children who may have been abused may express their sad, negative or angry feelings through their behaviour. Children do not always have the words to express the feelings they have, especially about something as momentous as abuse. They may be afraid to discuss the abuse or feel that discussing it may make matters worse. A child who has been abused may have a great deal to cope with, including changes in their home situation and the reactions of those around them. These children may express their unhappy feelings through difficult behaviour, in the same ways that many unhappy children do. The types of difficult behaviour you may find in school are: aggression, out-bursts and tantrums; swearing, rudeness, verbal aggression; physical assaults on other children or adults; truanting, leaving school without authorization; crying, shouting or becoming hysterical; withdrawal, avoiding other children and adults, isolation; refusing to respond to requests or instructions; and disrupting classes.

In some cases the child may become very challenging and a serious management problem. For many children this process is about their feelings of low self-worth and their need to challenge others to see if they are still valued. Managing this behaviour requires both firmness and recognition of the underlying causes.

## *Handling difficult behaviour*

Strategies to handle this type of behaviour include:

♦ staying calm and cool

♦ acknowledging the child is distressed

♦ trying to get the child away from other children when there is an incident

♦ distinguishing between the child and the child's unwanted behaviour

♦ remaining supportive and accepting of the child

♦ praising wanted behaviour and positive actions on the child's part

♦ giving the child responsibility and a chance to succeed

♦ never trying to pretend that the abuse has not happened or that it is in the past

♦ being dependable and reliable in the child's life

♦ reassuring the child that he is an important and valued member of the class

♦ sharing strategies for supporting the child with parents and other professionals involved with the child.

It is possible that you may not have been involved in the abuse enquiry relating to a particular child and you may have little information about his situation. This can make it difficult to respond effectively to the child's behaviour. However, it is important to recognize that a child in this situation is not just being 'naughty' but may be struggling with real despair and some very distressing feelings.

## *Helping with low self-esteem and lack of confidence*

It is common for children who have been abused to suffer from low self-esteem and to lack confidence in many situations. Self-esteem develops in children from the experiences they have and the responses they get from others. Abused children have usually experienced negative responses from those closest to them, resulting in them often feeling unlovable and worthless. Depending on the type and severity of the abuse, the child may see herself as valueless, not belonging, not wanted, unacceptable or even evil. She may feel that she was abused because she was not good enough or because she deserved to be hurt. Sexually abused children may see their value only in terms of the sexual gratification they can give to adults.

Helping children develop improved self esteem and better confidence can be a slow process, requiring a consistent and patient approach. However, improvements in this area can be a key to helping the child move on from the abusive experience. Children with low self-esteem may: be sad, depressed, or withdrawn; lack confidence in tackling new tasks or refuse to do this; have low expectations of self; disrupt or become angry when faced with new tasks; show anxiety, panic or cry when faced with unfamiliar situations; feel a failure, and believe they cannot achieve; compare themselves unfavourably to others; and find it difficult to make and maintain friendships.

Strategies to help the child improve self-esteem need to be embedded in the work done in class and in activities around the school. All adults in contact with the child need to be positive and consistent in their approach and to recognize that the child has special needs in school. However, it is important that praise and recognition of achievements should be genuine, as abused children can be sensitive to lack of honesty or untrustworthiness in the adults around them. You can help a child who has been abused to improve self-esteem by:

♦ showing warmth and respect for the child

♦ being consistent, setting limitations

♦ providing opportunities for the child to genuinely succeed

- give the child opportunities to make decisions for himself

- giving the child responsibilities within her capabilities

- modelling positive behaviour towards the child in front of other children

- giving genuine praise and acknowledgement of achievements

- dealing sensitively with difficult behaviour

- listening to the child

- being genuine, trustworthy and reliable

- sharing concerns and strategies with parents and other professionals.

There may be many opportunities within the day for the child to be encouraged to act independently and to achieve. However, it is important that you progress at the child's pace and do not expect too much too soon.

## Helping the child with friendship

Abused children often feel isolated from those around them, having had experiences that they may simply not want to share with other children. Joining in conversations about home and family may be painful for a child who lives away from home or is separated from an abusive parent. Children may feel and be branded as 'different' because of their abusive experiences. Low self-esteem, withdrawal or disruptive behaviour may add to the problems an abused child may have in making and keeping friendships with other children. Children who are 'looked after' may experience more than one change in placements and may have moved school each time they moved to new carers. Some of these children may stop trying to fit in and make friends because they fear another disruptive move.

The result may be poor social confidence, lack of friendships or superficial, short-lived friendships and even isolation. The majority of children who are abused have problems making and keeping rewarding relationships.

If the child is struggling with social issues and seems to be having difficulty with friendships or becoming isolated, you could consider:

◆ discussing friendship and supporting others in circle time

◆ creating a 'circle of friends' to play with the child at breaks

◆ giving the child responsibilities in partnership with others

◆ modelling positive behaviour towards the child

◆ dealing with disruptive behaviour sensitively

◆ working to improve self-esteem.

Children who have been abused may be bullied or become bullies depending on their experiences, their character and personality, and the type and extent of their abuse. Bullying incidents should be dealt with as usual according to school policy. However, it is important that the child's situation and the events that have lead to it are considered and relevant support built into the response.

# Helping the child to learn

A child who has been abused may suffer delays or setbacks in her learning for a multitude of reasons, although this does not apply to all children who suffer abuse. Some of the reasons are: missing school; lack of support for education in the home; poor communication in the home; lack of appropriate toys, books and games; few new experiences; lack of pre-school provision; lack of confidence, low self-esteem; fear, pain and anxiety affecting concentration; tiredness, hunger, cold; and social withdrawal or isolation.

Supporting the child with her learning can be particularly difficult when events in the family have been distressing or traumatic. The child may find it hard to concentrate or enjoy learning when she is anxious, sad or angry about events outside school. Many abused children suffer delays in their learning and their achievement is affected. Some strategies for helping are:

♦ monitoring the child's effort and progress closely

♦ ensuring that the child is able to do the work set

♦ placing the child in a supportive group or pair

♦ letting the child do familiar work at an easier level at particularly stressful times

♦ not pressurising the child when she is angry, worried or sad

♦ trying to involve the child in choices of tasks, materials or books

♦ giving deserved praise and rewards

♦ getting support from appropriate others, e.g. the SENCO, LEA Special Needs service.

## *Working with other professionals to support the child*

It is likely that you will not be the only professional involved with the child in the aftermath of abuse. A social worker, at least, will probably be assigned to the child and family as their key worker and there may be others involved in working to support them. This could include health staff, therapists as described above, voluntary sector organizations and possibly specialist education staff. You may be part of the 'core group' which develops the child protection plan and ensures that the child's safety and welfare are monitored. The child protection plan may assign the school a particular role in supporting the child. It is crucial that professionals working with a family co-ordinate their efforts and communicate effectively with each other. In order to promote effective working together you should:

♦ be clear what is expected of you in your role within the child protection plan

- know who the key worker is and communicate any concerns you may have to him

- work with the CPLT to ensure that the aims of the child protection plan are met

- ask for support from others in school if you are concerned about the child

- where possible talk to other professionals involved with the child

- attend review child protection case conferences (within your school's policy on this)

- keep records of any concerns you have about the child

- maintain confidentiality.

Every child who has suffered abuse will respond differently, making it difficult to generalize about how you can help. Perhaps the most important skill you bring to this situation is your knowledge of children's needs and the individual child, and your day-to-day positive regard and concern for the child.

# A whole-school approach to protecting children

Many of the responsibilities of schools outlined in *Working Together* involve the development of whole-school strategies to create a non-abusive environment for children. These include a general responsibility for the pastoral care of children and a responsibility to ensure that policies and procedures are in place for protection children.

## *Ensuring that school is a safe environment*

There are a number of principles on which to base creating a sense of safety for children in school. In this context, 'safety' refers to children's emotional and psychological sense of security as well as physical safety. In order for children to experience school as a safe environment, they need to feel:

♦ safe from physical harm, threats and bullying

♦ safe from fear, anxiety and anticipation of these feelings

♦ safe from verbal abuse, sarcasm and ridicule

♦ as if they belong to and are valued within the school

♦ as if their contributions are recognized and rewarded with acknowledgement and praise

♦ as if they can experiment, make mistakes and not be criticized for this

♦ as if they are making progress and achieving

♦ as if their particular type of family, first language, religion and culture are significantly acknowledged and accepted in the school environment.

Clearly, achieving a permanent sense of safety for all children at all times is a tall order! Children can feel unsafe if they quarrel with their best friend or lose their dinner money or fail to understand the tasks set. However, it is possible to help the children to feel safe most of the time through consideration of a number of issues:

♦ regularly using curriculum and PSE activities to promote respect for all within the school regardless of differences in background and ability

♦ ensuring that materials present positive images of all types of children and families

♦ ensuring that incidents of bullying are dealt with positively and promptly within school policy

♦ ensuring that incidents of racism are dealt with positively and promptly within school policy

♦ being sure that verbal assaults, name calling and other verbal forms of bullying or racism are taken as seriously as physical attacks

♦ using 'circle time' and other discussion venues to promote anti-racism and anti-bullying behaviour

♦ giving children tasks and responsibilities which promote positive self-image and create a sense of worth

♦ being pro-active in encouraging the children to reflect on their own behaviour, support each other and seek positive solutions to problems

♦ sharing strategies with colleagues

♦ ensuring parents are aware of school policy and practice in this area.

# Working with children who may have been abused

Children will respond to the prevailing ethos of the environment they are in, and perhaps the most important factor in determining their behaviour is the behaviour of the adults around them.

## *Using the curriculum to promote child safety*

There is a great deal of scope within the curriculum to explore issues with children about how different situations make them feel and what is and is not acceptable behaviour from one individual to another. There are also some specific schemes for addressing abuse issues within school, such as 'Kidscape Good Sense Defense' founded in 1986 by Michelle Elliott and Wendy Tidman. Programmes such as these tend to focus on:

- basic safe behaviour, e.g. not going off with strangers
- raising children's awareness of danger in the environment
- building self-confidence
- practical strategies for children to cope with potential abuse
- helping children to trust their own judgement
- teaching children to break the rules to protect themselves.

Raising awareness of potential dangers through the curriculum needs to be part of a whole-school strategy addressing these issues. Parents need to be in agreement with the school about how these matters are approached and there should be a strategy to ensure that materials are introduced at age-appropriate levels.

## Allegations of abuse against teachers

In a recent discussions with students on degree courses about working with children, the author asked the students to think about various practices in schools and nurseries where they were on placement, and to judge who was being protected by these rules. The practices included male students in an infant school being told not to touch children at all; female students being told not to sit a pre-school child on their knees unless they had a cushion on it; and a five-year-old cleaning and dressing a bad graze himself so the teacher did not have to touch him.

The students concluded that these practices and many others like them were designed to protect staff against allegations of abuse, rather than protect children against being abused. Clearly, touching children or having physical contact with them is not always inappropriate, and those of us who are parents may be disturbed to think that our injured school-child may not get a much-needed cuddle! So how can we get the balance right between protecting children and protecting adults from unfounded allegations of abuse? Whitney (1996: 97) argues that schools that deal effectively with allegations of abuse are often 'child protecting schools', and that the two things go hand in hand. He states that:

*Schools which are thorough about the protection of children will, I believe, also offer teachers effective protection against malicious or unreasonable allegations and be able to identify those cases which do give rise to genuine concern.*

It is important to acknowledge that children are abused in schools and that such abuse can take years to come to light; in some cases, it can be submerged for ever. Key issues in ensuring that both children and teachers are protected are:

♦ access to child protection training for teachers both before and after qualification

♦ commitment to child protection within the school, reflected in access to training, discussion of procedures, availability of key documents

♦ the willingness of colleagues to report suspicions of abuse by a teacher

♦ the development of procedures for dealing with allegations against teachers

♦ open and transparent decision-making processes

♦ support available for the child and the teacher.

Allegations against teachers are dealt with through the same procedures as any other child protection enquiry. Within any enquiry the child's welfare is seen as the paramount consideration, but this does not mean that teachers are automatically found 'guilty' if an allegation is made.

Procedures when an allegation is made should include:

♦ ascertaining if the complaint has any foundation

♦ assessing the extent of risk to pupils

♦ contacting social services to make a referral if there are grounds to do so

♦ considering if there is need to suspend the teacher for their own and the child's protection during the enquiry.

Normally, the headteacher will follow these procedures, but if the complaint is against the head, the governors must do this. Child protection procedures are then followed as in any other case.

Making an allegation against a colleague can be a great responsibility. Despite the protection of procedures, and legal and union representation, it is easy to believe that a colleague's career and reputation will never recover even if the allegation is groundless. However, if you have sufficient evidence to suggest that a colleague is involved in abuse it is vital that this information is passed on. In many of the fairly recent child abuse enquiries in residential care units, it was clear that colleagues had been aware of abuse but had not acted or not been believed, leaving future generations of children vulnerable to further abuse. Teachers who believe that a colleague may be involved in abuse of a child or children in the school should record their concerns and the details, including times and places, of any incidents; make note of any conversation with a child which includes an allegation of abuse; discuss their concerns with the headteacher; and maintain a high level of confidentiality.

## Checklist for action

♦ Ensure you are familiar with relevant school policies such as behaviour, racial harassment and bullying.

♦ Check the procedures within school for dealing with allegations of abuse against teachers.

♦ Check materials in school for supporting the development of children's self-protection and school policy on this.

♦ Share strategies with colleagues for supporting children's self-esteem and raising self-confidence.

♦ Consider how you can use the curriculum to develop children's sense of respect for themselves and others.

**6**

# Conclusion

Protecting children from abuse is a complex and demanding task for all professionals involved with children. Awareness of your own and other's roles is vital in ensuring that you take appropriate action to help children where abuse may have taken place. The role of teachers in child protection is expanding, and currently there is scope for changes in how child protection services are delivered, which may place schools in a much more central position in the process. In many ways, schools are ideally placed as a focus for the delivery of a much wider range of services and as a key point for developing better multi-agency strategies to protect children.

Developing skills in working with other professionals and recognizing the indicators of abuse through accessing child protection training is the first step in ensuring you can perform your role effectively. However, teachers increasingly need to ensure they have the skills to communicate with emotionally distressed children and support 'children in need' within school, to help abused children recover their self-confidence, and to support their social and emotional development as well as their learning. Hopefully, this short book has been a useful starting point.

Good luck!

# References

Baginsky, M. (2000), *Child Protection and Education.* London: NSPCC.

*Children Act 1989.* London: HMSO.

DHSS (1985), *A Child in Trust: Jasmine Beckford* (The Jasmine Beckford Report). London: HMSO.

DHSS (1987), *A Child in Mind: Protection of Children in a Responsible Society* (The Kimberley Carlisle Report). London: HMSO.

DoH (1999), *Working Together to Safeguard Children.* www.doh.gov.uk

DoH (2000), *Framework of Assessment of Children in Need and their Families.* London: HMSO; www.doh.gov.uk

DoH (2001), *Children and Young People on Child Protection Registers* – Year End 31 March 2001, England. London: HMSO; www.doh.gov.uk

NSPCC (2000), *Child Maltreatment in the United Kingdom.* Reported in the *Independent on Sunday*, 19/11/2000.

Revell, P. (2003), 'Your part in the war on abuse.' *TES* 7/2/03; www.tes.co.uk

Shaw, M. (2003), 'Share and save a child's life'. *TES* 31/1/03; www.tes.co.uk

*The Victoria Climbie Inquiry – Report of an Inquiry by Lord Laming* (January 2003). Crown Copyright; www.victoria-climbie-inquiry.org.uk